PRAYERS MY CATS
HAVE TAUGHT ME

CAT PSALMS
Prayers My Cats Have Taught Me

Large-quantity purchases or custom editions of this book are available at a discount from the publisher. For more information, contact the sales department at Augsburg Fortress, Publishers, 1-800-328-4648, or write to: Sales Director, Augsburg Fortress, Publishers, P.O. Box 1209, Minneapolis, MN 55440-1209.

ISBN 0-8066-4498-2

Cover and book design by Michelle L. N. Cook
Cover and interior art from Artville

The paper used in this publication meets the minimum requirements of American National Standard for Information Sciences—Permanence of Paper for Printed Library Materials, ANSI Z329.48-1984. ♾ ™

Manufactured in the U.S.A.

07   06   05   04   03   1   2   3   4   5   6   7   8   9   10

HERBERT BROKERING

PRAYERS MY CATS HAVE TAUGHT ME

Cat Psalms

Augsburg Books
MINNEAPOLIS

Dedicated to cats who have helped me pray:
Peveley
Kitty Black
Tinkie
Petsy
Tiger
Tiger II
Teewee
Machant
Dudley
Buffey
Alex
Tetra

CONTENTS

Introduction: Cats help me pray

I learn from metaphors: I look at one thing and understand another thing in myself. I am like a lily of the field, a sower who went out to sow, a wind in trees, bread broken, a mustard seed.

Most often I am like the cat.

In cats I see images of myself, of my soul. I watch a cat at peace, and I feel peace. I see a cat leaping gracefully, and my spirit leaps. *Cat Psalms* is about cats and the spirit. We find meaning in nature and spirit.

Cats have always been part of my life. I do not remember not knowing a cat in my seventy-five years.

I've known farm cats, alley cats, house cats. Mostly I grew up knowing barn cats whose kittens would run and hide if a stranger got near. But they knew us. They took the milk we brought them, they let us touch them, tame them. I was learning about my spirit.

On our Nebraska farm we came inside when the sun went down. Our cats went outside into the dark, unafraid. I wondered what they knew of the night that I would never see. My spirit, too, wanted to prowl in the dark.

I married a cat lover. On our long honeymoon drive to West Virginia, Lois and I were given a kitten in a Nebraska filling station—our first cat. As it grew up, that cat became a companion for our children—the first of many Cat Brokerings. The cats who lived and died in our home were friends and members of the family.

Our four children made clothes for the cats, built them houses, provided toys, taught them games, cuddled in bed with them on winter nights. The cats told us things about each other and ourselves.

Today our children no longer live with us. Now Lois and I have Alex and Tetra. One is a very white cat, one very black. Tetra peers through long black fur with round yellow eyes as though he has been all places in the universe. He looks wise, sometimes distant, sometimes sulky. In the morning Tetra waits for the door of the basement to open. Lois opens the door for him. Tetra thinks Lois is God.

Alex stands like a white Egyptian statue, waiting for a morsel and purring. He looks at us and begins to purr. He is sick and he purrs. He is chastised and soon purrs. Alex is a purring machine.

Tetra and Alex follow us nervously when we pack for a trip. They miss us when we are gone and are glad when we return. In Tetra and Alex we learn about curiosity, affection, anger, love, awe, contentment, elegance. They show me my spirit, my moods; they show me how I am with my master.

Cat Psalms is a book about what I learned from cats I have known. *Cat Psalms* are prayers of my spirit, my soul. Each psalm expresses an observation about a cat's nature (in the voice of the cat), followed by a prayer in which my spirit speaks of its cat-like nature to God.

My cats have taught me how to pray more deeply, with more imagination and understanding. This book is for all who seek to deepen their own prayer lives, imaging through nature. May the psalms give you fresh ways to see yourselves and new ways to pray.

Herbert Brokering

I am elegant.

I am Princess. I am Prince.
See me hold my head high
as I walk, as though I wear a
velvet scarf, a gold necklace,
a sapphire bracelet, a crown.
They cannot tell I am old. I
have heard them guess at my age. For a while I do not ache. And
then I prance and leap. And they guess me young. When they look
away, slowly I settle into my basket and curl and snuggle. I breathe
through my age and feel good years draw over me like a warm
blanket. I am old. I am tired. But when I hold my head high, when
I walk with careful grace, they guess me young.

O God,

You clothe my soul in fine raiment. Your promises are as soft as silk and precious jewels. I walk with my head high for all to see. I am young though I am old; for your blessings clothe me in elegance. They will see me, if but for a second, as elegant. I will show the gifts of my royal side, and they will know who lies curled quietly, breathing evenly, snuggled inside a royal soul dressed in your likeness.

Listen to me purr.

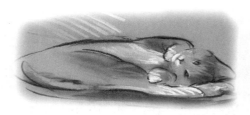

I purr.
Sometimes they do not hear.
Sometimes they stop talking,
look my way, smile. They
are sure they made me purr. Perhaps they did. I cannot always tell
where and why my purring begins. Purring is a sound that comes
when I am at home, inside, and don't need to go anywhere else—
when I am warm and content. It comes when they pet me and
tickle my chin. It is not easy to purr when someone is chasing me,
or if I am lost or cold or wet. I purr best when someone I know well
and trust is with me.

Dear God,

You give my soul a sound of its own, a language not in the dictionary. Its tune cannot be forced or commanded. My soul will sing when it must, when it decides from deep inside. My soul breathes songs and anthems with no words. All my good thoughts are in one sound; they repeat like the refrain of a hymn, a mantra. The peaceful sound of my soul is mine by heart. It stops. I look and listen to find it again. It begins where it left off. My soul purrs at the twinkle of the eye. My soul's purr is a lullaby, a pastel painting, a soft cotton cover. My soul's purr vibrates breath, life, spirit. Dear God, it is so when I let you rock my soul.

I have many moods.

I am cat. I have many moods.

I show all feelings, all emotions. My moods shift from moment to moment. Sometimes I am not easy to love, and will not be held. When they call I do not hear, and will not turn my head to them. Sometimes I will close my eyes and do not notice. Sometimes I will hiss or snap. When I choose, I will come to the ones I know and be loved by them. Then I show my great emotion, my love: I hold the one holding me. We will not let each other go, until I decide to leave. To those I trust I will return to lie at their feet. Again, I will be held and I will hold.

O God,

My soul is a pendulum, swinging from dark to light to dusk to dawn. I go in all directions. I come and I leave. I will not always be held. I leave the one who loves me best. I hear and do not respond; I want and do not show that I do. I am kissed and do not kiss back. I cannot find peace in my solitary night walks. My soul wanders, stays inside a hiding place. Sometimes I love and cannot quit.

Show me my center. Keep me at rest in your lap, caress my soul. A pendulum swings from the center of my soul. Dear God, you are the center.

One life is not enough.

I have nine lives.
*Some of these may be spent
already, but I do not keep
count. I live as though all
nine are still owed me. I will outlive my vets and the neighbors'
dogs. I could do without shots and pills and the pokes and prods of
the vet. But sometimes there's no getting out of it. And I try.
Sometimes I don't swallow the pill when they push it in my mouth,
but the taste is there—a bitter taste. They say I almost got run over.
It may be true, but I don't remember such things. Even so, I have
eight more lives. I will take more chances. Humans say, "You only
go around once." I will go around nine times. Maybe more.*

O God,

You give my soul long life. My soul began before I became the "me" I know. It will not quit when the "me" dies. I have been saved in daytime and in darkness. I live only for each day, and suddenly years have passed. I look at my years, and see decades go by. I long for more days and nights, and you let me grow old. My birthdays come more and more quickly. My times grow shorter as I grow older. A long life is full of your wonders. I will live through more than nine lives. I will be saved more than nine times ninety. My soul will live forever with you. Dear God, there is no end to your life in me.

Let me snuggle.

I need to snuggle.
I demand it. I push and
paw. I butt my head
against them. This is who
I am. I touch them, they
touch me back. They pet me, I pet them back. They make me glad,
I bless them. I purr, they feel the purr in themselves. The snuggle
is in my eyes. I am at their feet; I leap up beside them. Close, close.
I reach out on purpose as they pass by. I jump into their lap, not
caring if I shed, not caring if their fine clothing turns white or
black from my hair. Snuggling does not worry about being careful.
I honor them with my snuggle. I indulge them by being close. My
best spirit comes when I am held. But not too tight.

O God,

My soul has warm feelings. It needs holding and caressing. My soul will not be soul if it is left alone and untouched by others. It must touch and be touched. It must be held closely by you. My soul knows how to be held close—not too tightly, just right. My soul looks for you, for your life. We hold on together. My soul looks for others to hold. I snuggle. Intimacy can take many shapes and distances. But it is not careful of boundaries and cautions. O God, my soul must be close, must snuggle, must touch you and others to live. When far away, I need to be held. I want to feel your life. Close. Close.

Am I in your way?

I lie in their way.
They walk around me. I sleep, and they carefully step over my body. They do not harm me when I am most vulnerable. I lie in the open, where they come and go. I am a member of the family. I let them know when I am there. I put myself in their way: I sleep where they walk, lie where they would sit. I put myself under their feet; and they keep from harming me. I lie in their way so they will know I am here, so they will be careful of me. They know I trust them; they step over me.

O God,

My soul lies down in the way of those whom I trust. They know I am here; they step over me, around me—not on me. My soul is at peace in heavy traffic of friends. I will not lie in the way of those who would do me harm. I find places where my soul can rest and not be harmed. My friends know I am here. They know my need for rest; they know I need to be among them but at peace. They protect me. My soul finds rest in the open, in the presence of those who love me. I close my eyes where I will not be harmed. Dear God, notice me: I lie down in your presence, in your way. Dear God, I am here.

I choose what I want.

I know what I like.
If a food isn't right I
won't eat it. When they
change a brand I can
tell. If I like it, I will eat
it; if I do not like it, it will stay in my bowl. My taste buds are
demanding. Once I decide, I am stubborn. I am cat, I choose.
They can't tell me where to walk or sit or play. I will choose. I
cannot be pushed or pulled or coaxed or threatened. When I
decide they will know. Sometimes they wait and wait to see me
make up my mind. I will never be led on a leash. I can be chased
but I will decide where to run, how far to climb, how long to stay
away, and when to come back.

Dear God,

I am willful. I choose what to like or dislike. My will is strong, stubborn. I want to decide where I will be and work and play. I want to choose my friends and enemies—where to go and not to go. Threats and coaxing will only make me more stubborn, more sure that my way is right—even when it leads to disaster.

Inside my soul a voice says listen. Inside, your spirit seeks to guide the direction of my will. My soul speaks to me of your presence, your promise. My soul is alive, growing, unfolding in me. And I cannot ignore it. Dear God you made soul to be my self. Thank you.

The night is my friend.

I see in the dark.
My eyes open and let in
light. There is no darkness
too deep for me. I go out
when the sun has set. I sleep
by day, I prowl in the dark.
I do not grow tired in the dark. My eyes are like the moon, and
there are no clouds that hide my seeing. The night is when I am cat
the most. They do not follow me into the night. They stay behind,
wondering where I go, what I see, what I do. They sleep. I am alive
in the night. I see in the dark.

O God,

My soul prowls in the night. In darkness I see what I cannot see by light. My soul pierces darkness, the night cannot cloud its sight. When my day is clouded by darkness, by pain, by sorrow, by despair, my soul's eyes open and let in light. I see through clouds, I find stars and moon. I walk through shadows found only at night. My soul sees with eyes made for darkness. O God, you gave me a soul with night eyes. My soul can see distant light. Looking inward I see into your beyond. My soul plays in the shadow of your wings. O God, my soul sees light on the other side of darkness.

Don't forget about my needs.

I depend on them.
They think I rule the
house. I jump up to places
where I am not supposed
to be. They look for paw marks on the table, hair on the sofa. They
think I can do anything. They do not understand. I need their
help—though I hate to admit this. I cannot turn doorknobs to go in
and out at will. I cannot open cat food cans or pour milk from a
carton. The doors are closed. The refrigerator is shut. The food is
sealed in cans and bags. There is no live food to capture, the bird-
cage is locked. The toilet seat is down and I thirst. I must lower
myself to ask. They call me independent, but I depend on them. If
they go away or forget me, I could die. My life depends on them.

Dear God,

I depend on you. I cannot reach all I need. I cannot open clouds for rain, summon the morning sun or the moon by night. I cannot bring the end of day or form the mountains. I cannot call forth seasons in their order. The key to my life is hidden from me, the door to the future is locked. My soul must ask. I am born asking—for food, for comfort, to be held, for life. I am born needing love and trust, joy and family. I cannot find all I need, or keep it. My soul reaches out, takes, licks the bowl clean, waits for more. I depend on you, O God. My soul looks to you—and a door is unlocked, food is opened, water poured, bread broken. There is help, so I ask.

I stare without blinking.

I stare.

I cannot hear my breath. I am a living statue—only looking, looking at, looking through. They cannot know what I see, if I breathe. My eyes stay wide open while I stare. I do not blink. I do not turn. I look straight ahead. What I see does not see me. I want it, will have it. The window separates me from it, from having it. I seize what I see with my eyes.

I am cat; I stare and do not blink. I know what I see. They watch me, only I know.

O God,

My soul stares. My soul sees without moving, not blinking, only watching, waiting, wishing. I take what I see in this silence—city, mountain, valley, friend, sunrise, nighttime. It is mine. It is yours. And there is more. Sometimes the eye of my soul stares inward, to what was; or to the distance, to what may come. My soul sees what I feel, want, know. I seize it in my staring: my mountain, my valley, my fear, my love, my story, my miracle. All comes from you, O God. When my soul stares, I feel awe.

Approach my things with care.

I will claw, fight, bite to defend my cat rights.
I will protect myself and keep my things safe—for myself. I will strike, chase, stalk, scratch. I will make sounds of anger, power, threat. I will scream. I have named my territory, it is mine. Those who come to see me need permission. This is my room, my corner, my basket, my bow, my yard. I will raise my back, make my hair stand up, scream my warnings. I will defend what is mine alone.

O God,

My soul will fight, defend, protect what is mine. My soul loves the life you have given me. I want my space, my time alone, my time with you, my holy place, my own room. I will not be destroyed, abandoned, lost. I will not let anything steal away my faith, my love, my honor, my home. My soul will scratch, howl, chase, risk—and defeat. I will not be beaten because you are strong within me. I may be hurt and wounded, I may bleed and suffer, I may grow weary and weak. But I will not lose what is mine, O God. I want your life in me.

Treats are always welcome.

I love gifts, a cat present.
Fresh catnip will do for a
start. Or a tiny ball that
rolls fast, or a toy they name "mouse." Leftover turkey is also good.
Sometimes they give me a collar with a bell and bow. And they
smile proudly. I will allow this, though turkey is better. I will be
pretty for them until I tire of the feel. Then I will scratch at my
neck. When they talk softly and kindly to each other, that is a gift
to me. I notice voice sounds. They rent a video on cats, read a cat
book, and they look at me and smile. That is their gift. The best
present is to sit very close to them when we are alone, hearing
music, reading, being near. With my eyes shut I feel them look at
me with love. Being together is the gift.

Dear God,

I like gifts: a ring, a sweater, a book, a framed picture, candy. A night out is a gift, or a new toy, a gold bracelet, slippers. A bright sunrise, a soft breeze, a friend's call, being close to you— these bring joy. The best gift is the giving, the way you give to me, your generous spirit, your love. My soul loves the giving more than the tinted wrapping, more than sapphire, more than gold inside. What you give is homemade. You make what I need, you want it for me, you wrap it and give it to me. Giving is your great gift. See me: see how I want, take, open, wear, keep your gifts. Dear God, show me my gift-wrapped world.

I do not like changes.

I notice changes.

When they change the furniture, I can tell. If an empty bag is left on the floor, I look inside. When there's a sandwich on the counter, I jump, look, sniff, investigate. When company comes, I examine them. I know if they've been near another cat, even before they tell each other. If they move my sleeping basket, it takes me longer to get settled. I can tell when they're packing to leave. Then I hear the car coming in the driveway. When they change my brand of cat food I know immediately. If they want to give me a pill, I can tell by the way they move, the way they look at me. I know it's time to hide. I notice when something is different. It slows me down, changes my plans. I am careful when something big changes.

O God,

My soul knows when seasons turn, when birds migrate,
when skies turn dark or fill with snow. My soul knows when
someone near me is hurting or bursting with pride. I can tell
when a friend no longer cares for me. I can feel when
something doesn't get said, or is spoken without meaning.
I know when something changes even when I cannot see. My
soul knows when my life is changing. You know that I know.
I have learned to live with changes, but they slow me down,
make me look twice. I peek into something new on tiptoe.
My soul plays hide and seek inside some secret paper bag.
O God, you made my soul to know the difference between
what was and is.

Leave me alone.

I need alone time.
I need to be all by myself, where
I choose, and when. I do not plan
solitude in advance; but when it
comes, it will be as long as I choose. I will decide. Right now you
must leave me alone. You want to hold me, pet me, get me to play
with string or a ball of paper. Not now.

I am not walking away because I don't love you. This is my
little downtime. Perhaps I will nap, curl up in one place until
being alone is done. Being alone is necessary; it is when I sort
through cat things. The world will stop when I stop. Nothing will
happen without my making it happen. You will have to wait for me.
This is my time-out.

O God,

My soul needs solitude, being by itself with you, stillness to muse, coast, ponder in the heart. I schedule time alone—early morning alone, late at night alone. I withdraw to a secret place from time to time. I must build solitude into my life. You know my spirit and its needs: I may be moody, sad, tired, frustrated, or elated. I need to be with myself and apart from others. Solitude is a time for getting strength, letting the world go by, resting, not being in control, taking what is given. O God, your quiet is always here, your presence always near. Solitude is my exercise for peace, trust, cleansing, being myself. O God, there is so much in your quiet for the whole world to hear.

Don't laugh at me.

I can have my feelings hurt.

It can happen when I walk into a window by accident. I am embarrassed. I act like it didn't happen. If I slip on a waxed floor, or lose my balance and miss a leap, I hope no one is looking. If I tip my milk bowl over, I pretend I did not do it, or that I did it on purpose. I lick up the milk as though it's easier this way. I do not want their angry words, I do not like blame or shame.

Sometimes I need to tear through the house—a sudden dash across the room, a bounce off the wall, a leap onto a table. Then I am finished; I am elegant once more. This always surprises them, makes them point and laugh. I do not like this. Then I get cranky and sulk. I walk away. Cats are not to be laughed at. Cats have dignity.

Dear God,

I am easily embarrassed. I do not like being laughed at.
Sometimes I will bump into a thing that's right before my
eyes, or forget a name I know by heart, or blunder when
guests are watching. My soul likes to be right, to be admired,
respected. I like being at my best. It is hard to forgive myself
when I am clumsy or foolish or wrong. I am quick to blame
others, to feel blamed, to show shame. You know this about
me, you know how I am. I can strike back, run away, hide,
sulk. I can act as though I did nothing wrong, or that it is not
my fault. O God, you know how I am. Teach me to laugh at
myself. Teach me to love myself.

I will wait for what I want.

I can wait.

They make me wait for things. I must wait while they decide. They decide what I need, what I want, what I will have. Sometimes I wait without looking. Sometimes I wait staring at them, looking up at them. I wait expecting something good—a tasty snack, dinner, a toy, a pat, a scratch under my neck, an open door. They surprise me. I receive what I did not know was in the refrigerator, on the counter, in the cupboard. I wait with hope. I wait as a cat must wait and wait and wait. Waiting is more than begging. When I wait, I expect, I long for, I count on them. I sit still and wait to be rewarded. Or I touch them, cry out, rub against them. I make sure they know I am there, waiting. They notice my waiting, and they are impressed.

O God,

I wait for you. Help me to wait believing. I wait for what I can never reach, never make, never deserve. I wait even for what I do not know is there. Waiting opens tomorrow, or now, or forever. Waiting keeps a horizon before my soul. Waiting grows inside me, unfolding, opening, expecting, receiving. I wait as a bud waits for the root to open the bloom. I wait for what was and will be. I wait to be sure of what is. Waiting is the joy of not yet having, not yet seeing, and learning to believe. My soul waits, learning to be sure of you. O God, my soul waits for what you promise is already here.

Curiosity will not kill me.

I am filled with curiosity.
Anything they are doing
I want to know about. I
watch to see what they are making and how it will turn out and if
I can help. I want to know what they are reading and how it feels
beneath my paws. I wonder whom their phone call is from and if
I can add my sounds to theirs.

My curiosity is strongest when I see them opening a box. I move
in close. If I am close they will notice me and show me. If they
leave the room, I will investigate on my own. I want to be next to
the box, on top of the box, inside the box. There is so much to see,
to discover. I want to know what's next, who is here, what is there.
They help me be curious. Curiosity keeps me alive, makes me a cat.

O God,

I am curious. I seek and knock, I wait and watch. I want to know what you are doing with my world, with my life—how it will turn out, if I can help. I examine what is far, what is near, what is done, what will come. I have so many questions; there is so much I do not understand. I must know. Finding out puts my soul in the middle of how I see you, hear you, believe you. My soul begs to comprehend. My soul searches in the dark, listens in the silence, is curious in the morning watch. O God, you made so much to watch, to discover, to care for, to hope for. Curiosity will not kill me; it will keep me alive.

Your love is welcome.

Hold me.

Kiss me. Snuggle me. I am a cat. Talk to me softly, in whispers. Stroke me with your fingertips and look into my face. Say my name. Repeat soothing words again and again. Ask me whatever you want. Tell me I am special, beautiful, elegant. Make your voice loving, caressing, admiring. Adore me. Be glad for me. Say how much I mean to you, what you will do for me. Stretch the truth; exaggerate your love. Show me your heart. Tell me who I am when I am good. Tell me I am very good. Say I am your best friend. Adore me. I am a cat.

Dear God,

I need so much love. My soul wants to be held, reassured, admired, wanted. My soul will grow strong if it is held close, be quieted if it is kissed, become joyful if it is forgiven. I need your love. Caress my soul with your heart, with your voice, your promise, your grace. May I come to know you as my best friend, my soul friend. Dear God, you know how my soul was created in love and how it needs love to live—now and beyond this life. Your love is here without asking. My soul comes from you, and it breathes your love like air, feels your love like a touch, hears your love as a whisper. My soul is well when your love is its life.

The world is full of smells.

I know through my nose.
They hurry past me with
leftover turkey; I knew they
were coming two rooms away. I am awake, on my feet, following
every step. My nose tells me this is something I like. I do not follow
grapefruit or carrots unless I think there may be chicken or ham in
the same bowl. I know fish through walls; its scent can wake me out
of a deep sleep. I sniff the air and follow the smell. I come to the fish
and expect them to share. Just a bit will do, though I will always ask
for more. It isn't how much they give me, because even a tiny bite
will leave its smell on me. And then I have fish wherever I go. My
world is a feast of smells. I wash my face and paws. I am satisfied.

Dear God,

My soul knows the aroma of seasons. Your blossoms of spring
are sweet smelling, autumn leaves have a whiff of age and soft
decay. Winter's cold sharpness carries the scent of wood fires.
Each aroma wakens a time inside me and floods me with
memories. Aromas of home stay within me. A smell, a taste, a
whiff, and suddenly my soul recalls meals and flowers and
people—images of long ago. My soul is filled with aromas of
places and times of year. Dear God, your April breeze quiets
me with fragrance of new bloom. The scent of candle flame
can make my soul stretch, wake in awe, sing. My soul begs for
a morsel of all that is sweet smelling. You have filled the earth
with incense; it is my home.

Let me in, let me out.

I get to change my mind.
They let me out, I need to come
in. I didn't see the dog out
there. I didn't know it was
raining. I smell food inside.

Now I want out. I need to see if the dog has left, if the rain has
stopped. They won't give me any of the food. It is boring inside.

In and out, out and in, all day long. It's enough to keep a cat
busy. They wouldn't let me in and out here if they didn't want to.
When I'm let in, I hope I can I can remember what I want; other-
wise I'll ask to go back out. I always need to ask them. I can't open
the door myself.

O God,

My soul wants out. My soul must get away, someplace new. I need space, air, adventure. When I am out, my soul wants back in. It longs for rest, warmth, the safety of home. O God, let me hear a voice I know, an aroma, a word of welcome.

Again my soul wants out, one more time to be gone, to get away, to seek what is new and exciting. Let me out, Lord. My soul needs a vacation, time off, a break.

O God, now I've been gone long enough, longer than I wanted. Let me back in. I need someone I know.

I want in, I want out. In and out. Be patient with me. Be with me—inside and out.

In an instant I am awake.

I wake quickly.
Even when I sleep
soundly, one eye inside me is alert, peeking. In an instant I wake
from a sound sleep, and I am ready. I can be a night cat awake or a
morning cat awake. Once awake I am ready to do what I must in
that moment. I can be wakened by a door opening, a waft of food,
a motor, footsteps, any strange sound. While asleep I am on call, on
alert, on duty. I do not want to miss any sound that might affect
me. If it is not important, I peek quickly and go back to sleep. If the
sound is important, it becomes a bugle call: I am on my feet, ready
to do my duty, ready to be cat. Sometimes I blink, stretch, yawn.
I wake slowly, carefully. But when necessary, I can wake in the
batting of an eye. I know when.

O God,

My soul is always on alert. When it seems deep in sleep, my soul can be wakened in a moment. While asleep my soul is resting and ready, at peace and alert. I can be wakened by sudden fright or delight. A wish or dream will wake me to test the wish, to live the dream. I can be wakened instantly, ready to fight, ready to rise and claim a promise. My soul is quick to react, faster than a word spoken, swifter than a feeling. When your alarm clock rings within me, my soul is wide-awake. O God, you created my soul to wake quickly and seize life.

I am fierce, I am frightened.

I am frightened.
Suddenly my eyes open
wide, the hairs on my back
and on my tail stand up.
My ears pull back against my head. I am afraid, but I will look
fierce. I am a warrior, even if afraid. I will prepare to defend
myself, to defend my rights. Even if I choose not to fight, even if I
choose to run, I first will make myself fierce—like a tiger or leop-
ard. I will hiss and spit and snarl. I will growl like a lion. Look at
me: I have grown bigger, more dangerous. I arch my back, my tail
swings like a weapon. I am ready to do battle—or to run. I am a
frightened cat. I am a dangerous cat. When the fear leaves me, I
will be their cat again.

O God,

My soul knows fright. My soul changes size and shape when I am afraid. It becomes a force, a sword, a spear, a weapon. My soul is my shield and protection. It prepares to hold off the enemy—or to flee, if it must. My fright mixes with fierceness in my eyes, in my posture, my face, my words. I raise my voice, I make brave sounds, pretend to be stronger than I am. If I cannot fight and be strong, I will run. I must decide when it is wise to fight or to flee. My soul draws its courage and wisdom from you. I learn from my fear. You will guard me from evil, harm, and foe. You will teach me to fight or to flee.

Let me sleep, let me sleep.

I am cat; I sleep.

I sleep long, short, deep, light. I know all ways to sleep. And I sleep often. I breathe slowly, quietly; my belly rises and falls with my breath. They watch me sleep when they are awake. They know I sleep often, sleep well. When it is time, I draw my body into a circle, put my head on my paws, shut one eye, two eyes, sleep. My body goes limp. I do not stir. They wonder how I can sleep so soon, so deep, so often. Awake, I lick my paws, my sides, my ears; then I turn and go back to sleep. I dream of stalking birds, leaping, climbing, chasing. My whiskers twitch, my body twitches with my dreams. They smile as they watch me sleep and dream. They want my world of sleep. My heart is quiet. I am warm, I am loved. There is no enemy. I am cat, and I sleep well.

Dear God,

I long for sleep. My body rests, wakes, frets, tosses, slumbers, sleeps. Night is sometimes long, sometimes sleepless. My soul prays for rest. Day is done, work is finished; I close the shades, let go of my plans and cares. I think of you. I give you my day, my work, my thoughts, my cares. My soul stretches, yawns. I quit climbing mountains, I trust deep valleys, I forgive the enemy. I love. I sleep. My soul rests in the night. You have given me the gift of sleep. My rest is in your peace. Dear God, you made my soul to rest, to lie down in green pastures, beside still waters. You restore me in sleep and peace.

I choose my own space.

I choose where I want to be.
They give me a box with a
towel, I choose a chair. They
give me a chair, I choose a rug.
I decide on my place to be. Also
I like the chair at the end of the
table. Its velvet cushion becomes
my new place. They cannot sit
in this chair while I lie there.

    My basket with the plaid blanket has been moved. I want it
back. I step in and out of the basket a hundred times a day. It must
be placed by the window once more, so I can look outdoors. I find
another place—the sunny spot on the living room rug. I move
across the rug with the afternoon sun. The sun is warming my spot
on the rug. I will want the recliner at times, too. They will not
choose for me. I am a cat; I choose my own space.

Dear God,

My soul chooses where it wants to be, where it needs to stay, where it feels at home. My blanket, my basket, my spot of sun, my velvet pillow, my cozy recliner. I have my own places, each suited for a mood, thought, dream, need. These are homes for my soul, places where I always am welcome. I go to my soul homes to lie down, receive love and strength, be renewed. My soul knows where to go when I need to reflect, be content, seek forgiveness, forgive. Dear God, you have made many homes for me and in these places you fill my soul with love and warmth. You have made life so I may choose spaces for my soul.

Thank you and please.

I am grateful.

See me give thanks. I rub against their legs, purr, look into their faces, and thank. They know when I give thanks. My thanks are always followed by "please." I can make them sound alike. If they won't give me more, I walk away as if satisfied, lick my paws, wash my face, and pretend it was a feast. But I am washing for the next course. I am ready in case more is coming. My giving thanks may be rewarded. I will give thanks, even if nothing more comes. A cat can be grateful. But they have been good to me; they will be good to me again. "Thank you" and "more, please." I am their cat, they are mine. I am thankful, I expect more.

Oh God,

My soul is thankful. I cannot thank you enough for all there is for me. I wish I could thank more and ask less. I give thanks immediately, or later, or sometimes never. But I am thankful. When I give thanks, I belong. Thanking reminds me that you care about me, love me. Thanking shows me I have more than enough. When I thank, I also say "please." Thank you for this, please keep it coming. O God, you have seated me at a very great table, a table that never goes empty. My soul gives thanks, for there is always more, so many second helpings. Dear God, there is room for others at that table. When I give thanks I will pass it on, I will share.

Silence surrounds me.

I walk without making a sound.

My paws move like fog, I hold my breath inside every step. I build silence around me when I walk. Soft sounds around me are stilled when I approach. I cannot hear myself move. Silence is inside me. I am at peace. My steps are careful; dry leaves become cotton beneath my paws. The place I am grows quiet. They cannot hear me. They do not know if I am near. The silence is my strength, my power. I will not be rushed. My feet glide and leap with grace, with purpose. I do not feel my motion. I am powered from within. I know silence. I am cat, walking still. There is no sound.

O God,

My soul is still. I breathe without seeming to take a breath. All around me is hushed. You fill my silence with peace and love. My soul grows quiet without trying. Inside I am wide-awake, alert. My soul floats on clouds. I walk in mid-air, my feet and head in heaven and on earth. I move on wings, I fly to you. All sound vanishes as I approach, nothing can enter my silence. Nothing but your still presence. I walk in silence, listening only for your voice, your peace. I am covered in silence. I am at rest. O God, my soul is covered with your peace. My soul is still.